M000317800

Miami Hurricanes IQ: The Ultimate Test of True Fandom

CRAIG T. SMITH

Printed in the United States of America.
Copyright © 2013 by Craig T. Smith.

This title is part of the IQ Sports History / Trivia Series, which is a trademark owned by Black Mesa Publishing, LLC.

Cataloging-in-Publication Data is available from the Library of Congress.

ISBN: 978-0-9912699-0-7
First edition, first printing.

Front cover photo courtesy of Matthew Zipay. Back cover stadium photo courtesy of Erica Cecich. Special thanks to Kathryn Murphy. All other photos and cover design by Holly Walden Ross.

Black Mesa Publishing, LLC
Florida

www.blackmesabooks.com

BLACK MESA IQ TITLES

Mixed Martial Arts (Vol. 1 & 2)
Atlanta Braves
New York Yankees
Georgia Bulldogs
Boston Celtics (Vol. 1 & 2)
Florida Gators
Milwaukee Brewers
St. Louis Cardinals (Vol. 1 & 2)
Major League Baseball
Boston Red Sox (Vol. 1 & 2)
Tampa Bay Rays
Oklahoma Sooners
Texas Longhorns
Texas A&M Aggies
Cincinnati Reds
New England Patriots
West Point
Rock & Roll Music
Buffalo Bills
Kentucky Derby
NHL Hockey
The Beatles
Cleveland Indians
Miami Hurricanes
Baltimore Orioles
Green Bay Packers

Miami Hurricanes

CONTENTS

INTRODUCTION   1

TWO-A-DAYS   5

FIRST HALF   13

SECOND HALF   37

THE RESULTS   63

ABOUT THE AUTHOR   65

BLACK MESA PUBLISHING   67

INTRODUCTION

The University of Miami football history has followed one of the more unusual paths that a major college program could follow. Through ebbs and flows with moderate successes on a national scale, the program still remained known as a vacation spot for major powers as much as it did for its football for decades. After all, the nickname Suntan U wasn't stumbled upon by accident. In fact, the program was even close to being terminated by the administration in the late 70s.

Then, a man, a pipe, and a five-year plan saved the University of Miami football program. The inroads of hard work were laid on the practice fields, and after five seasons, Howard Schnellenberger had not only followed through on his promise to win a national championship in five years, but also had established Miami as a top program on the rise. Four national championships in nine years proved that to be true. Swagger was born (after all, it necessitated the "Miami Rule" in 1990), and a new national power had been born.

While this book is about celebrating the greatness of Miami's highest achievements, it's also to recognize the ample foundation that was laid by countless many former Canes over decades prior. I hope you enjoy the ride and find that this book rekindles some of those great memories you experienced in years past, as well as push your knowledge of the Canes' history to the absolute limit. Good luck!

Craig T. Smith
J.D. 2004, University of Miami

"For every year of greatness there is usually three years of preparation. We have to go through the battlefields of Kansas, Oklahoma, Minnesota and Louisville to get to where we need to go. We'll take casualties and bloodlettings along the way, but we'll get there faster than if we take the high road."
— Howard Schnellenberger

TWO-A-DAYS

Here's your big chance. It's a sweltering August morning on the Greentree Practice Fields at the University of Miami, as a hungry group of Hurricanes gets ready to take another run at championship aspirations. This is where you get your chance to show that you know some simple fundamentals about Hurricane football and the University of Miami. Although this book will focus on everything associated with the Miami program, we'll just toss you a grab bag of softballs here. We aren't going to push you too terribly hard, yet. After all, you'll need to have something left in the tank when we ratchet up the difficulty of the questions later in the book. Wouldn't exactly look good to the administration to see everyone dropping off like flies in the first few pages, now would it?

As you look around you, know that you stand in the midst of a program that has enjoyed a lion's share of successes in the past three decades, but is also a program that has a rich history. A head coach who hung up his clipboard and whistle and went overseas to fight in World War II, then picked them back up and continued to hammer his players after two years of service. The gruff, baritone-voiced Schnellenberger who bellied out his teachings learned under Bear Bryant to his players between puffs of smoke on the practice field. And yes, the booming voice of Michael Irvin issuing challenges at any and all teammates, freshman or veteran.

You are standing on the field where so many winning lessons in football and life have been taught. Cherish this opportunity to show what you can do. So, without further ado, it's time to blow the whistle and see if you're cut out for the tough life of a football (trivia) superstar … or if we'll be seeing you waving a foam finger as the team rolls by on the bus headed for Sun Life Stadium for a Labor Day weekend kickoff. Enjoy!

Question 1: The Hurricanes have two Heisman Trophy winners in their illustrious history. Name the winners, and the year they won the trophy.

Question 2: The Hurricanes have won five national championships in their history. Which of the following years did they *not* win the title?
>   a) 1983
>   b) 1987
>   c) 1988
>   d) 1989

Question 3: Before slamming opponents in the squared circle, this professional wrestling icon was a letterman as a Hurricane defensive lineman from 1992 to 1994. Who is he?

Question 4: When Jimmy Johnson was hired as head coach in 1984 to replace the recently departed Howard Schnellenberger, from what school did he leave?
>   a) Oklahoma
>   b) Tulsa
>   c) Oklahoma State
>   d) Arkansas

Question 5: Miami's 58-game home winning streak still remains the longest in college football history. In what years did the streak start and end?
   a) 1981; 1992
   b) 1982; 1995
   c) 1984; 1993
   d) 1985; 1994

Question 6: The Ibis was selected as the school's first unofficial mascot in 1926. Why did school officials select it?
   a) It was the first animal to leave before a storm hit the area, and the first to return after the storm passed
   b) It was a bird found all over campus
   c) It was the favorite pet of one of the school's founding administrators
   d) It was found on the practice field while the football team was practicing and would not leave

Question 7: In the 2001 Sugar Bowl, the Canes pulled away from the Gators late for a 37-20 win, getting the better of their in-state rival in the "Brawl on Bourbon Street". Who was the game MVP?
   a) Jeremy Shockey
   b) Ken Dorsey
   c) Najeh Davenport
   d) Clinton Portis

Question 8: Coach Howard Schnellenberger was known for having a deep, gruff voice, sporting a suit on the sideline, and smoking a…what?

Question 9: Freshman phenom Randy "Duke" Johnson exploded on the scene for the Canes in 2012, totaling 2,060 all-purpose yards. He came 48 yards short of matching the record for all-purpose yards gained in a season by this current pro Cane.

a) Andre Johnson
b) Devin Hester
c) Frank Gore
d) Willis McGahee

Question 10: The University of Miami has inducted 16 former players into its Ring of Honor. As of 2013, which of the following has *not* been named to the Ring of Honor?
a) Edgerrin James
b) Ray Lewis
c) Ottis Anderson
d) George Mira, Sr.

Question 11: In 1991, despite going 12-0 and shutting out Nebraska 22-0 in the Orange Bowl, the Hurricanes split the national championship. Who did they "share" the title with?
a) Nebraska
b) Colorado
c) USC
d) Washington

Question 12: The Orange Bowl Stadium opened in 1937. What was the original name of the stadium?
a) Roddy Burdine Municipal Stadium
b) Hurricane Stadium
c) Sunrise Stadium
d) City Stadium

Question 13: This former Hurricane wide receiver helped Miami win two national championships, but was perhaps more known for his brash on-field behavior. Who was memorialized in college football lore during his last game as a Cane—a 46-3 win over Texas in the Cotton Bowl—when he scored a touchdown, ran up the tunnel, and walked back firing imaginary six-shooters at the Longhorn players?
a) Michael Irvin

b) Lamar Thomas
c) Randal Hill
d) Brett Perriman

Question 14: In a series known for failed kicks, this was the original. Trailing Miami 17-16 late in the fourth quarter at Doak Campbell Stadium, FSU's Casey Weldon mounted a furious last minute drive, giving this kicker a chance to beat the Canes from 34 yards out. What was the name of this kicker that pushed the kick wide, creating "Wide Right I"?
a) Dan Mowrey
b) Gerry Thomas
c) Matt Munyon
d) Xavier Beitia

Question 15: Edgerrin James holds the school record for most rushing yards in a game, with a bruising performance against the third-ranked and undefeated UCLA Bruins on December 5, 1998. "The Edge" ran over the UCLA defense, carrying the ball 39 times (which also tied the school record) en route to a shocking 49-45 come-from-behind win that knocked the Bruins out of the national championship game. How many yards did James run for on the day?
a) 268
b) 284
c) 299
d) 312

Question 16: This Hurricane tailback shattered the school record books in 2002 in a number of categories, including total rushing yards for a season, rushing attempts for a season, rushing touchdowns in a season, and average rushing yards per game in a season. Who is he?
a) Willis McGahee
b) Frank Gore
c) Clinton Portis

d) Najeh Davenport

Question 17: After finishing my Hurricane career with a national championship in 1987, I was drafted by the Cowboys with their first pick of the 1988 draft. I made five straight Pro Bowls, won three Super Bowl Rings, and set an NFL record in 1995 with eleven 100-yard receiving games. Who am I?

Question 18: Miami has won five AP national championships, which puts them into a tie for fourth most all-time. Who are they tied with?
  a) Michigan
  b) USC
  c) Oklahoma
  d) Nebraska

Question 19: In 1989, top-ranked Notre Dame and Miami met in the Orange Bowl in the final week of the regular season. Leading 17-10 in the third quarter, the Miami offense faced a third and what seemed to be a mile after a 15-yard penalty, a Craig Erickson fumble, and a running attempt. Erickson took the snap and lobbed a ball deep down the sideline to Randal Hill for an improbable first down conversion that helped carry the Canes to a 27-10 victory on their way to their third national championship in seven years. How many yards did the Canes have to go to convert that third down?
  a) 29
  b) 35
  c) 43
  d) 45

Question 20: This former Hurricane great was inducted into the Pro Football Hall of Fame on August 3, 2013. He helped redefine the defensive tackle position, terrorizing quarterbacks as a Buccaneer and Raider during a thirteen-year NFL career. Who is he?

TWO-A-DAYS ANSWER KEY
(1-20)

1. Vinny Testaverde – 1986; Gino Torretta – 1992
2. C
3. Dwayne "The Rock" Johnson
4. C
5. D
6. A
7. B
8. Pipe
9. D
10. B
11. D
12. A
13. C
14. B
15. C
16. A
17. Michael Irvin
18. B
19. C
20. Warren Sapp

"The difference between ordinary and extraordinary is that little extra."
— Jimmy Johnson

FIRST HALF

So you've made it through the sweltering two-a-days, and you're ready to take on a full-fledged set of demanding trivia questions to show Al Golden, Art Kehoe and company that you have what it takes to become the next Miami football (trivia) legend at the U.

Sitting at your locker, you can hear the feet pounding on the concrete above as the fans anticipate the greatest entrance in football: the run through the smoke. The click-clack of dozens of cleats is drowned out by the noise of the crowd, which crescendos as you walk down the tunnel toward the field. As you stop at the mouth of the "U" helmet, players jump around, banging into each other, waiting to erupt. The fire extinguishers billow smoke, Sebastian raises the American flag, and Al Golden yells, "Let's go, men!" You take the field, ready to show that all the preparation, from game watching to record searching, has made you the ultimate wealth of orange-and-green-based sports information.

Question 21: With three of them in 2012, QB Stephen Morris set the school record for most 400+ yard passing games in a

season, and in the process tied which former Cane quarterback for most in a career?
- a) Vinny Testaverde
- b) Steve Walsh
- c) Bernie Kosar
- d) Gino Torretta

Question 22: Trailing Miami 31-24 late in the fourth quarter of the 1984 Orange Bowl, Nebraska QB Turner Gill led the Cornhuskers on a last minute drive deep into Miami territory. On fourth and eight from the 24, Gill pitched to I-back Jeff Smith, who found the end zone. Coach Tom Osborne elected to go for two and the win. Gill's pass was batted away in the end zone by a Miami defender, preserving the win and Miami's first national championship. Who was the defender who broke up the pass?
- a) Reggie Sutton
- b) Troy White
- c) Jay Brophy
- d) Kenny Calhoun

Question 23: When did the Ibis mascot first make an appearance at a Miami football game?
- a) 1950
- b) 1955
- c) 1958
- d) 1981

Question 24: A follow up question: how did "Sebastian" the Ibis get his name?
- a) He's named after the first person to play him
- b) It was the name given to a real ibis by the members of the Miami zoo
- c) It was the name selected by a student vote
- d) The original person who portrayed the Ibis lived in San Sebastian Hall, a former university dormitory

Question 25: In the 1981 season opener against Florida, this current SEC head coach came on for starting QB Jim Kelly, who left the game with a calf injury. Trailing 20-11, this individual helped engineer two scoring drives, the second of which ended with a Danny Miller 55-yard field goal to give Miami a 21-20 victory over their in-state rival. Who was this former Canes quarterback?

Question 26: The Canes joined the Big East Conference in 1991 after fifty years of being an independent. What previous conference / association were they a member of?
  a) Southern Intercollegiate Athletic Association
  b) Atlantic Central Football Conference
  c) Dixie Conference
  d) Eastern Collegiate Football Conference

Question 27: Miami won its first game 7-0 in 1926. Who did they beat?
  a) Amherst College
  b) James Madison University
  c) Temple University
  d) Rollins College

Question 28: Miami started the 1989 season with a 51-3 blowout win on the road at a current Big Ten member school. Which team was humiliated at home by the Canes?
  a) Michigan
  b) Michigan State
  c) Wisconsin
  d) Iowa

Question 29: Miami has an 18-16 all-time bowl record. The most bowl games against any one opponent for the Canes is six. Which team has opposed the Canes more than any other in a bowl game?
  a) Notre Dame

b) Alabama
c) Nebraska
d) Oklahoma

Question 30: This long-time school relic is fired off after the team entrance and after every score at a Miami home game. What is the name of this relic?
a) Canes Cannon
b) Touchdown Tommy
c) Old Thunder
d) Sebastian's Cannon

Question 31: This hard-hitting linebacker terrorized the middle of the field, taking home the school's only Dick Butkus Award Trophy. Who is he?
a) Ray Lewis
b) Jonathan Vilma
c) Micheal Barrow
d) Dan Morgan

Question 32: Miami has ended four opponents' winning streaks of 20 or more games, one of only two schools to ever do so. Which of the following schools most recently had a streak snapped by the Canes?
a) UCLA
b) Nebraska
c) Oklahoma
d) Notre Dame

Question 33: In 2001, Miami set a modern NCAA record for combined margin of victory in consecutive games against ranked opponents, with dominating performances against Syracuse and Washington in the Orange Bowl. What was the combined score of those games?
a) 110-14
b) 124-7

c) 113-0
d) 119-7

Question 34: An original member of Big East Conference, how many times did the Canes finish first or tied for first in the conference in their thirteen years of Big East football?
a) 6
b) 8
c) 9
d) 11

Question 35: Who was MVP of the 1992 Orange Bowl?
a) Gino Torretta
b) Larry Jones
c) Kevin Williams
d) Lamar Thomas

Question 36: In 1992, FSU's Tamarick Vanover was the victim of a devastating hit in the game known as Wide Right II. Which Miami defender delivered the shot?
a) Micheal Barrow
b) Jessie Armstead
c) Ryan McNeil
d) Darrin Smith

Question 37: Miami played in the most watched college football game in ESPN history. Which game was it?
a) 2006 vs. FSU
b) 2008 vs. Florida
c) 2009 vs. FSU
d) 1986 vs. Oklahoma

Question 38: Miami has had numerous All-Americans, but only one player in school history has won the honor three times. Who was he?
a) Ray Lewis

　　b) Ted Hendricks
　　c) Bryant McKinnie
　　d) Michael Irvin

Question 39: Which season was Dennis Erickson's last as Miami's head coach?
　　a) 1992
　　b) 1993
　　c) 1994
　　d) 1995

Question 40: I was born in Jefferson, Louisiana and was a two-time All-American, helping to lead Miami to a national championship. In addition to starring on the football field, I also won the Big East championship for the javelin throw. I was drafted in the first round and have a Super Bowl ring. Who am I?

FIRST HALF ANSWER KEY
(21-40)

21. D
22. D
23. C
24. D
25. Mark Richt
26. A
27. D
28. C
29. C
30. B
31. D
32. A
33. B
34. C
35. B
36. A
37. A
38. B
39. C
40. Ed Reed

Question 41: In the 2003 Fiesta Bowl/National Championship Game, what official threw a controversial flag for pass interference on fourth down that kept the game alive for Ohio State?

    a) Terry Porter
    b) Randy Christal
    c) Dennis Hennigan
    d) Al Matthews

Question 42: During this national championship season, Miami defeated five teams ranked in the AP Top 10. What year was it?

    a) 1983
    b) 1987
    c) 1991
    d) 2001

Question 43: This former Miami quarterback was a two-time All-American and is a member of the Hurricanes ring of honor. He is also remembered for his game-winning touchdown with his non-throwing hand to beat the Gators in the Swamp. Who is he?

    a) Bernie Kosar
    b) Jim Kelly
    c) Vinny Testaverde
    d) George Mira, Sr.

Question 44: This tailback became the first Hurricane running back to rush for 1,000 yards. He was drafted eighth overall by the Arizona Cardinals and highlighted a 14-year NFL career with the NFL Rookie of the Year award, as well as MVP honors in Super Bowl XXV. Who is he?

    a) Alonzo Highsmith
    b) Warren Williams
    c) Ottis Anderson
    d) Albert Bentley

Question 45: Jim Kelly threw for 280 yards and three touchdowns as the Canes defeated this ranked opponent 26-10 in Kelly's first career start as Miami's QB.
   a) Nebraska
   b) Penn State
   c) Florida
   d) Notre Dame

Question 46: In 2002, Willis McGahee set the school record for rushing touchdowns in one game in a 56-45 win over Virginia Tech that clinched a spot in the Fiesta Bowl/National Championship Game. How many times did he find the end zone?
   a) 4
   b) 5
   c) 6
   d) 7

Question 47: This former walk-on kicker from Coral Gables led the Hurricanes in scoring during his four-year career in which he established an NCAA record for PATs made (157). He is still the school's all-time leader in field goals made (73) and PATs made (178). He was inducted into the University of Miami Sports Hall of Fame. Who is he?
   a) Carlos Huerta
   b) Dane Prewitt
   c) Todd Sievers
   d) Andy Crosland

Question 48: From 1997-2000, this future NFL star set a school record with 4,384 career all-purpose yards.
   a) Santana Moss
   b) Edgerrin James
   c) Clinton Portis
   d) Reggie Wayne

Question 49: Which quarterback succeeded Jim Kelly as starter?
  a) Vinny Testaverde
  b) Bernie Kosar
  c) Craig Erickson
  d) Steve Walsh

Question 50: This defensive great has the most career fumble recoveries in UM history.
  a) Ted Hendricks
  b) Ray Lewis
  c) Dan Morgan
  d) Ed Reed

Question 51: Who caught the game winning touchdown from Ken Dorsey in Miami's thrilling come-from-behind victory over FSU in 2000?
  a) Santana Moss
  b) Najeh Davenport
  c) Reggie Wayne
  d) Jeremy Shockey

Question 52: This future NFL star began his UM career as a running back before converting to linebacker, where he was drafted in the first round by the Denver Broncos.
  a) Jonathan Vilma
  b) Dan Morgan
  c) DJ Williams
  d) Randy Shannon

Question 53: Which UM offensive lineman was most recently awarded All-American honors?
  a) Joaquin Gonzalez
  b) Bryant McKinnie
  c) Brett Romberg
  d) Eric Winston

Question 54: In Miami's thrilling 38-33 comeback win over the Gators in 2003, this electrifying return man took the opening kickoff the distance for an early 7-0 lead.
a) Sinorice Moss
b) Antrel Rolle
c) Devin Hester
d) Sean Taylor

Question 55: This former Canes head coach was a First-Team All-American QB for UM in 1959, as well as an academic All-American.
a) Fran Curci
b) Lou Saban
c) Andy Gustafson
d) Howard Schnellenberger

Question 56: In 2004, Louisville led Miami 24-7 at half in the Orange Bowl, but Miami rallied for a 41-38 victory before a national audience on Thursday Night on ESPN. Who scored the winning touchdown with 0:49 remaining?
a) Greg Olsen
b) Roscoe Parish
c) Devin Hester
d) Frank Gore

Question 57: Miami has played Alabama 17 times in their history. When is their last victory over the Crimson Tide?
a) 1990 Sugar Bowl
b) 1993 Sugar Bowl
c) 1955 at Orange Bowl
d) 1979 at Tuscaloosa

Question 58: This tailback came on strong following a knee injury to Frank Gore and earned MVP honors in the 2004 Orange Bowl, rushing for 131 yards in Miami's 16-14 win over FSU.

a) Jason Geathers
b) Jarrett Payton
c) Tyrone Moss
d) Quadtrine Hill

Question 59: In 1997, Miami played its first ever overtime game. Who was the opponent?
a) Virginia Tech
b) Syracuse
c) Pittsburgh
d) Boston College

Question 60: When was the last time Miami defeated a #1 ranked team in the AP poll?
a) 1991 vs. Florida State
b) 1995 v. Nebraska
c) 1989 v. Notre Dame
d) 2000 v. Florida State

FIRST HALF ANSWER KEY
(41-60)

41. A
42. B
43. D
44. C
45. B
46. C
47. A
48. A
49. B
50. A
51. D
52. C
53. D
54. C
55. A
56. D
57. A
58. B
59. D
60. D

Question 61: Ken Dorsey is the winningest quarterback in UM history. What was his career record as a starter?
   a) 35-3
   b) 38-3
   c) 38-2
   d) 36-3

Question 62: In December 1966, this individual became the first African-American football player to sign with the University of Miami.
   a) Ray Bellamy
   b) Tom Sullivan
   c) Burgess Owens
   d) Chuck Foreman

Question 63: With trips to Japan, San Diego, Syracuse, and Penn State, Miami—who became known as the "Jet Lag Kids"—set an NCAA record for distance traveled in a season in 1979. Approximately how many miles did they travel?
   a) Up to 12,000
   b) 12,001 to 18,000
   c) 18,001 to 28,000
   d) More than 28,000

Question 64: Why did Howard Schnellenberger tack on a field-goal while leading 28-7 with seconds remaining at Florida Field in 1980?
   a) Students were pelting his players and coaches with frozen oranges
   b) To get back at Florida Coach Charley Pell for pregame comments
   c) To give his kicker practice for the upcoming Peach Bowl game
   d) To give UM the largest margin of victory ever at Florida Field

Question 65: Who caught the eventual game-winning touchdown pass from Steve Walsh in Miami's 26-25 comeback win over FSU in Tallahassee?
a) Brett Perriman
b) Melvin Bratton
c) Michael Irvin
d) Randal Hill

Question 66: Which of the following former UM head coaches did *not* hold a head coaching position with a current NFL franchise?
a) Lou Saban
b) Fran Curci
c) Jimmy Johnson
d) Butch Davis

Question 67: This current pro Cane led the NFL in catches (115) and receiving yards (1,575) in 2008.
a) Andre Johnson
b) Reggie Wayne
c) Santana Moss
d) Kellen Winslow, Jr.

Question 68: This year's Miami team set school records for total yards per game (482.9) and passing yards per game (324.8).
a) 1986
b) 2001
c) 2002
d) 1990

Question 69: I was a consensus All-American in 1990 and Outland Trophy winner, helping lead my team to two national championships in 1987 and 1989. I was the top overall pick in the 1991 NFL Draft and won three Super Bowl rings in my ten year NFL career. I was inducted to the college football and University of Miami sports halls of fame. Who am I?

Question 70: Leading the Gators 27-16 in the Swamp in 2002, this Hurricane defender stepped in front of a Rex Grossman pass and raced 97 yards for the score that put the game away in a 41-16 romp.
   a) Sean Taylor
   b) DJ Williams
   c) Kelly Jennings
   d) Maurice Sikes

Question 71: Miami vs. Florida State was the second of the "Big Three" to start an annual series. In what year did the schools first play?
   a) 1947
   b) 1951
   c) 1953
   d) 1958

Question 72: A follow up question—True or False: Florida State won its first matchup with the Canes.

Question 73: Who was the first rookie head coach since 1948 to lead his team to a national championship?
   a) Jimmy Johnson
   b) Dennis Erickson
   c) Howard Schnellenberger
   d) Larry Coker

Question 74: To instill the discipline he learned from coaching under Bear Bryant, this Schnellenberger morning ritual was considered a deterrent to breaking team rules.
   a) Sunrise Sprint Club
   b) The Breakfast Club
   c) Morning Madness
   d) The Puking Games

Question 75: Miami's longest streak of wins over FSU at Doak Campbell Stadium is currently four. What years does that win streak span?
  a) 1981-1983-1985-1987
  b) 1975-1977-1979-1981
  c) 1983-1985-1987-1989
  d) 1989-1991-1993-1995

Question 76: I was the Big East conference defensive player of the year in 2003. Who am I?
  a) Jonathan Vilma
  b) Vince Wilfork
  c) Sean Taylor
  d) DJ Williams

Question 77: Which of the following did *not* win the Maxwell Award?
  a) Ken Dorsey
  b) Jim Kelly
  c) Vinny Testaverde
  d) Gino Torretta

Question 78: In which of the following national championship games vs. Miami did an opponent *not* run the "Fumblerooski" play for a touchdown?
  a) 1984 Orange Bowl vs. Nebraska
  b) 1988 Orange Bowl vs. Oklahoma
  c) 1990 Sugar Bowl vs. Alabama
  d) It's never been done in a title game

Question 79: Who holds the UM coaching record with 93 wins?
  a) Dennis Erickson
  b) Lou Saban
  c) Andy Gustafson
  d) Jack Harding

Question 80: In what year was the school's famous "Split U" logo developed?

    a) 1966
    b) 1973
    c) 1975
    d) 1981

FIRST HALF ANSWER KEY
(61-80)

61. C
62. A
63. D
64. A
65. C
66. B
67. A
68. D
69. Russell Maryland
70. D
71. B
72. False – UM won 35-13 in the Orange Bowl
73. D
74. B
75. A
76. C
77. B
78. C
79. C
80. B

Question 81: This Hurricane player was shown kissing a Miami cheerleader after winning the 1988 Orange Bowl and the national championship, which graced the cover of the January 11, 1988 edition of Sports Illustrated.
a) Steve Walsh
b) Michael Irvin
c) Dennis Kelleher
d) George Mira, Jr.

Question 82: Miami switched from the block number uniform style to their current style of uniform in what year?
a) 1997
b) 1998
c) 2000
d) 2001

Question 83: Since winning the program's first national title in 1983, how many undefeated seasons has Miami posted?
a) 2
b) 3
c) 4
d) 5

Question 84: Miami scored two late touchdowns to snatch victory from the jaws of defeat in a nationally televised game on ESPN against Florida in 1984. At what neutral site was the game played?
a) Tampa
b) Jacksonville
c) Orlando
d) Atlanta

Question 85: What was the "State of Miami"?
a) The unofficial name given to Miami sweeping FSU and
   Florida in the same season

b) The recruiting area south of Orlando designated by
    Howard Schnellenberger as belonging to Miami
c) The Orange Bowl facility during the school's
    unprecedented 58-game winning streak
d) The wild and rambunctious state of play by Miami's
    flashy players during the 1980s

Question 86: Miami's final victory in the Orange Bowl Stadium
was against whom?
  a) Georgia Tech
  b) Virginia
  c) NC State
  d) Duke

Question 87: Bernie Kosar was the offensive MVP of the 1984
Orange Bowl. Which Miami defender earned defensive MVP
honors in the 1984 Orange Bowl?
  a) Ken Calhoun
  b) Jack Fernandez
  c) Tony Fitzgerald
  d) Jay Brophy

Question 88: How many times has Miami defeated the #1
ranked team in the AP poll?
  a) 5
  b) 7
  c) 9
  d) 12

Question 89: Miami players carried Larry Coker off the field
after his final game, an MPC Computers Bowl win to cap the
2006 season. Who did the Canes beat?
  a) Georgia Tech
  b) Boise State
  c) Nevada
  d) Michigan State

Question 90: Before being tapped as Dennis Erickson's replacement, Butch Davis was the defensive coordinator for which team?
a) Philadelphia Eagles
b) Cleveland Browns
c) New Orleans Saints
d) Dallas Cowboys

Question 91: Which of the following players has *not* been inducted into the Pro Football Hall of Fame as of 2013?
a) Michael Irvin
b) Ted Hendricks
c) Russell Maryland
d) Cortez Kennedy

Question 92: Which of the following future NFL running backs was *not* on the 2001 national championship team?
a) Clinton Portis
b) James Jackson
c) Frank Gore
d) Willis McGahee

Question 93: Who was the Seminole kicker that hooked the would-be game winning kick in the Orange Bowl against Miami in 2002, known as "Wide Left I"?
a) Dan Mowrey
b) Matt Munyon
c) Xavier Beitia
d) Gerry Thomas

Question 94: The Canes have had one Mackey Award winner in their history. Who is he?

Question 95: In 1989, Miami's defense, anchored by All-Americans Greg Mark and Cortez Kennedy, led the nation in

total defense and scoring defense. What were the yards/points allowed that the Canes' defense posted for the season?
a) 255.3 ypg; 15.5 ppg
b) 195.5 ypg; 7.1 ppg
c) 216.5 ypg; 9.3 ppg
d) 280.2 ypg; 12.5 ppg

Question 96: True or False: Miami dealt Steve Spurrier a loss in his final game at Florida Field as a player.

Question 97: Who won Big East Rookie of the Year honors in 1997 and set a school record for catches (48) by a freshman?
a) Reggie Wayne
b) Santana Moss
c) Andre King
d) Bubba Franks

Question 98: Florida and Miami is the oldest played rivalry between the state's "Big 3". In what year did they first play?
a) 1935
b) 1938
c) 1941
d) 1947

Question 99: Which former Miami tight end finished with the most career receiving yards at UM?
a) Bubba Franks
b) Jeremy Shockey
c) Kellen Winslow, Jr.
d) Greg Olsen

Question 100: Who is Miami's all-time leading rusher?
a) Frank Gore
b) Ottis Anderson
c) Clinton Portis
d) Stephen McGuire

FIRST HALF ANSWER KEY
(81-100)

81. C
82. C
83. B
84. A
85. B
86. D
87. B
88. C
89. C
90. D
91. C
92. B
93. C
94. Kellen Winslow, Jr.
95. C
96. True
97. A
98. B
99. C
100. B

"Discipline is a lot more than saying, 'Don't throw your hands up in the air when you score a touchdown.' Discipline is when it's 110 degrees in the Orange Bowl, no breeze, fourth quarter, a minute and a half left to play, fourth and three for the other team, you're dead tired, they come to the line, and that opposing quarterback gives you a hard count: 'Hut-HUT!' And you don't jump offside. Because you're disciplined mentally and physically."

— Michael Irvin

SECOND HALF

You're sitting on a bench in the locker room, towel over your head. Sweat drips from your brow, creating a streak of jet-black ink running down your face. You ache from head to toe. You've found out that this is no high school waltz; these questions hit hard, and maybe you've found yourself scratching your head and feeling lost too often. Maybe the feeling of inadequacy is starting to seep in your psyche. Heck, maybe you didn't realize there was this much to know about Miami football history.

But then you look at the locker next to yours and see a famous quote from the unflappable Michael Irvin that's posted around the locker room as a reminder to the focus and discipline it takes to succeed in Coral Gables.

Rejuvenated, you grab your helmet, crack your neck, slap Al Golden on the back, and jog back through the tunnel out to the field, ready to break down each question and give your all in the quest for the ultimate Miami sports fan trivia knowledge.

Question 101: This former Cane holds the school record for most career tackles with 532.

a) Dan Morgan
b) Ray Lewis
c) Bernard "Tiger" Clark
d) Jonathan Vilma

Question 102: Who was MVP of the 1990 Sugar Bowl?
a) Craig Erickson.
b) Stephen McGuire
c) Rob Chudzinski
d) Alex Johnson

Question 103: Following a 37-14 dismantling of the Cornhuskers in the 2002 BCS National Championship Game, the Hurricanes tied the 1968 USC Trojans for the most players taken in the first round of the NFL Draft (at that time). How many Canes were drafted?
a) 4
b) 5
c) 6
d) 7

Question 104: In Miami's last game against Michigan, Carlos Huerta nailed a late FG to win 31-30 in Ann Arbor. What year was this?
a) 1987
b) 1988
c) 1990
d) 1991

Question 105: True or False: Miami swept all-Big East awards for Offensive Player of the Year, Defensive Player of the Year, Special Teams Player of the Year, and Coach of the Year in 2000.

Question 106: In 1987, Miami trailed Florida State in Tallahassee before Steve Walsh engineered a furious comeback with three touchdown passes on the way to a 26-25 victory. From what deficit did Miami rally?

a) 14-3
b) 18-6
c) 19-3
d) 25-3

Question 107: What year was the last in the annual UM-Notre Dame rivalry?

a) 1988
b) 1989
c) 1990
d) 1991

Question 108: As of the end of the 2012 season, this WR holds the school record for catches in a season.

a) Santana Moss
b) Reggie Wayne
c) Andre Johnson
d) Leonard Hankerson

Question 109: This defensive lineman was known as the "Mad Stork".

a) Ted Hendricks
b) Jim Burt
c) Tony Fitzgerald
d) Dan Sileo

Question 110: This player returned a fumble by FSU quarterback Xavier Lee for the game-clinching TD at Doak Campbell stadium in 2007.

a) Tavares Gooden
b) Colin McCarthy
c) Allen Bailey
d) Kenny Phillips

Question 111: In which year did Miami *not* win the "State Championship" (vs. Florida and FSU)?
  a) 2000
  b) 2002
  c) 2004
  d) 2008

Question 112: In what year did Miami win its first ever officially recognized conference title?
  a) 1948
  b) 1951
  c) 1991
  d) 1994

Question 113: This individual served as athletic director at UM for 15 years and also compiled a 54-32-3 record as UM head coach.
  a) Fran Curci
  b) Jack Harding
  c) Andy Gustafson
  d) Charlie Tate

Question 114: When was Miami's first undefeated season?
  a) 1926
  b) 1950
  c) 1987
  d) 1989

Question 115: Miami ripped off a school record 34-game winning streak following a 34-29 road loss in the second week of the 2000 season to which of the following teams?
  a) Penn State
  b) Washington
  c) Nebraska
  d) Maryland

Question 116: Which of the following head coaches did *not* have a winning record against both UF and FSU?
   a) Jimmy Johnson
   b) Howard Schnellenberger
   c) Larry Coker
   d) Fran Curci

Question 117: Which of the following QBs had the most wins as a starter?
   a) Bernie Kosar
   b) Jim Kelly
   c) Ken Dorsey
   d) Vinny Testaverde

Question 118: This former Miami quarterback was inducted into the college football Hall of Fame in 1997 as a head coach at a different school, where he won a national championship and six conference titles. Who is he?
   a) Don James
   b) Fran Curci
   c) George Mira, Sr.
   d) Charlie Tate

Question 119: This was Miami's first All-American selection in 1950.
   a) Don James
   b) George Mira, Sr.
   c) Al Carapella
   d) Don Bosseler

Question 120: Who were co-MVPs of 2002 Rose Bowl?
   a) Ken Dorsey/Andre Johnson
   b) Ken Dorsey/Jeremy Shockey
   c) Ken Dorsey/Clinton Portis
   d) Jeremy Shockey/Jonathan Vilma

SECOND HALF ANSWER KEY
(101-120)

101. A
102. A
103. B
104. B
105. True
106. C
107. C
108. D
109. A
110. B
111. D
112. D
113. B
114. A
115. B
116. D
117. C
118. A
119. C
120. A

Question 121: A senior safety on the 1987 national championship team, I also won the Jim Thorpe Award in 1987 and was a Pro Bowler with the Detroit Lions in 1991. I was nominated to the College Football Hall of Fame in 2006 and the UM Ring of Honor in 2009. Who am I?

Question 122: Miami has played traditional powerhouse USC just twice in its history, with the first meeting taking place in Los Angeles in 1966. What was the result for Miami?
   a) L, 28-3
   b) W, 19-3
   c) L, 17-16
   d) W, 10-7

Question 123: Which of the following former Miami head coaches does *not* have a Super Bowl ring?
   a) Jimmy Johnson
   b) Butch Davis
   c) Howard Schnellenberger
   d) Lou Saban

Question 124: Beginning in 1953, Miami has played Virginia Tech 30 times in their history. Who leads the series, and by what count?
   a) Miami, 16-14
   b) Miami, 18-12
   c) Virginia Tech, 17-13
   d) Neither, series tied at 15

Question 125: How many times have Notre Dame and Miami faced off as #1 vs. #2 in the AP poll rankings?
   a) 1
   b) 2
   c) 3
   d) Never

Question 126: Miami won a school record thirteen-straight homecoming games through 1995. The streak was broken in 1996 by which team?
a) Florida State
b) Syracuse
c) Virginia Tech
d) West Virginia

Question 127: Sebastian the Ibis was briefly detained by police during the 1989 season for what offense?
a) Tackling the Irish mascot on the sideline
b) Attempting to put out the flame on Chief Osceola' spear
c) Running onto the field while a play was in progress
d) Snatching a hat off the head of an Alabama fan

Question 128: This former Miami star anchored the center of the Oakland Raider offensive line for fifteen years, and played in six AFC/AFL title games, as well as Super Bowl II. He is a member of the Pro Football Hall of Fame. Who is he?
a) Jim Burt
b) Jim Otto
c) Art Shell
d) Gene Upshaw

Question 129: I was a fullback for the Canes from 1953-1956, receiving AP All-American honors as a senior. I was drafted ninth overall in the 1957 NFL Draft and made the 1959 Pro Bowl during a seven-year NFL career. Who am I?
a) Don Bosseler
b) Eddie Dunn
c) Whitey Rouviere
d) Harry Mallios

Question 130: The 1989 Canes hold the school record for fewest punt returns allowed by opponents. What's the number?
a) 5

b) 9
c) 12
d) 15

Question 131: A follow up question: out of the few punt returns they allowed, the 1989 squad set an NCAA record for fewest punt return yards allowed. How many yards did they give up?
   a) 2
   b) 12
   c) 27
   d) 35

Question 132: Known for his hair, and his flair on the football field, this Miami legend and South Florida icon was inducted into the College Football Hall of Fame in 2012.
   a) Jimmy Johnson
   b) Howard Schnellenberger
   c) Dave Wannstedt
   d) Bernie Kosar

Question 133: In which season did Miami set a school record with 14 First-Team Big East all-conference selections?
   a) 1991
   b) 2000
   c) 2001
   d) 2002

Question 134: In 1992, trailing 19-16, Bobby Bowden elected to go for the tie instead of the win in the closing seconds. Who missed the field goal in Wide Right II?
   a) Xavier Beitia
   b) Dan Mowrey
   c) Gerry Thomas
   d) Matt Munyon

Question 135: True or False: Both Jimmy Johnson and Butch Davis were born in Arkansas.

Question 136: In what year was Miami's first televised game and who was the opponent?
a) 1959 at LSU
b) 1955 at Georgia Tech
c) 1955 vs. Notre Dame
d) 1961 vs. Penn State

Question 137: Who has the longest winning streak in the Miami-Florida series?
a) UF – 5
b) UM – 5
c) UF – 7
d) UM – 6

Question 138: True or False: Miami has a winning bowl record all-time.

Question 139: How many career touchdown passes did Bernie Kosar throw as a Cane?
a) 40
b) 42
c) 45
d) 35

Question 140: Against which of the following schools does Miami *not* have an all-time winning record?
a) Pittsburgh
b) Oklahoma
c) Florida
d) Penn State

SECOND HALF ANSWER KEY
(121-140)

121. Bennie Blades
122. D
123. D
124. B
125. D
126. C
127. B
128. B
129. A
130. C
131. A
132. A
133. C
134. B
135. False – Johnson was born in Port Arthur, TX; Davis in
    Talhequah, OK
136. B
137. C
138. True
139. A
140. D

Question 141: When was the last time the Canes were shut out?
a) 2003 vs. Tennessee
b) 2005 at FSU
c) 2006 vs. Georgia Tech
d) 2007 vs. Virginia

Question 142: In this non-championship season, Miami held the #1 ranking for 15 straight weeks and was televised in eight of their twelve games. What year was this?
a) 1984
b) 1990
c) 1986
d) 1992

Question 143: Who took a two-year break from coaching the Canes to serve in World War II?
a) Jack Harding
b) Irl Tubbs
c) Eddie Dunn
d) Andy Gustafson

Question 144: In 2001, who won the prestigious academic Heisman award? Peyton Manning (1997), Danny Wuerffel (1996), and Kyle Van den Bosch (2000) are other standouts on the football field and in the classroom who have won this award.
a) Ken Dorsey
b) Jonathan Vilma
c) Ed Reed
d) Joaquin Gonzalez

Question 145: This defensive lineman earned All-American honors as a senior in 1977, when he set a then-school record with 15 sacks.
a) George Halas
b) Don Latimer

c) Don Smith
d) Tony Galente

Question 146: In 1997, the Canes set a school record for most 300+ yard rushing games to start a season. How many times in a row did they do it?
   a) 2
   b) 3
   c) 4
   d) 5

Question 147: This running back boasts a Miami school record 90-yard touchdown run.
   a) Ottis Anderson
   b) Edgerrin James
   c) Alonzo Highsmith
   d) Jack Losch

Question 148: Name the current (2013) play-by-play announcer for the Canes on Miami's radio network.

Question 149: Who has the longest interception return for a touchdown in school history?
   a) Ed Reed
   b) Maurice Sikes
   c) Bennie Blades
   d) Selwyn Brown

Question 150: Known for his arm and pocket presence, how many career rushing touchdowns did Ken Dorsey tally at Miami?
   a) 0
   b) 2
   c) 4
   d) 5

Question 151: Who was the inaugural coach of the Miami football program?
  a) Jack Harding
  b) J. Burton Rix
  c) Howard P. Buck
  d) Irl Tubbs

Question 152: Which of the following were not on the starting offensive line for the 2001 national championship team?
  a) Brett Romberg
  b) Sherko Haji-Rasouli
  c) Bryant McKinnie
  d) Eric Winston

Question 153: Following a loss to Arizona in the Fiesta Bowl to end the 1993 season, Miami fell to 15th in the polls, marking the first time in how weeks that the Canes were not ranked in the Top 10?
  a) 95
  b) 112
  c) 137
  d) 151

Question 154: Which Miami squad became the first team in Big East history to record back-to-back shutouts with wins over Rutgers (33-0) and Pittsburgh (45-0)?
  a) 1991
  b) 1992
  c) 1996
  d) 2000

Question 155: After seeing his team score in the waning seconds to bring the Noles within 26-25 in Tallahassee in 1987, Bobby Bowden called for a two-point conversion, rather than play for the tie. Danny McManus's pass was knocked away to

preserve the 26-25 victory. Which defender saved the game for the Canes?
a) Bernard Clark
b) Bubba McDowell
c) Bennie Blades
d) Randy Shannon

Question 156: A 58-7 beating at the hands of the Canes in the Orange Bowl to end Notre Dame's season at 5-6 also ended the tenure of which former Irish head coach?
a) Gerry Faust
b) Ara Parseghian
c) Dan Devine
d) Lou Holtz

Question 157: Despite not being a member since the 2003 season, Miami dominates the number of combined Big East conference offensive and defensive players of the year with thirteen players. Who is the next closest school with nine combined players?
a) Virginia Tech
b) Syracuse
c) Rutgers
d) Pittsburgh

Question 158: This fullback on the 1989 and 1991 championship teams set the school record for career rushing touchdowns with 35. Who is he?
a) Albert Bentley
b) Stephen McGuire
c) Larry Jones
d) Leonard Conley

Question 159: Miami has gone the Junior College route to find a number of impact players. Which of the following was *not* a junior college transfer?

a) DE Jerome McDougle
b) QB Scott Covington
c) TE Jeremy Shockey
d) LT Bryant McKinnie

Question 160: Miami's all-time record as the #1 ranked team in the land in the AP Poll is:
a) 30-11
b) 28-7
c) 43-6
d) 31-7

SECOND HALF ANSWER KEY
(141-160)

141. D
142. C
143. A
144. D
145. B
146. B
147. D
148. Joe Zagacki
149. D
150. B
151. C
152. D
153. C
154. C
155. B
156. A
157. D
158. B
159. B
160. C

Question 161: True or False: Miami coach Andy Gustafson had a career winning record against the Florida Gators during his 16-year tenure.

Question 162: I was selected as an All-American three times at Miami. My fifteen-year NFL career included time with the Green Bay Packers, Baltimore Colts, and Oakland/Los Angeles Raiders. I was on four Super Bowl-winning teams and was named to the Pro Football Hall of Fame in 1990. Who am I?

Question 163: This defensive back holds the school record for both career tackles by a cornerback (120) and tackles in a season by a cornerback (73). Who is he?
a) Tolbert Bain
b) Tom Beier
c) Phillip Buchanon
d) Antrel Rolle

Question 164: This former First-Team All-American selection holds the school record for tackles in a season by a defensive tackle (98). Who is he?
a) Rubin Carter
b) Warren Sapp
c) Russell Maryland
d) Cortez Kennedy

Question 165: In 1950, in what was considered one of the biggest surprise wins in the school's early history, Miami went on the road and upset this present day Big Ten opponent 20-14, one week after it had ended Notre Dame's 39-game unbeaten streak.
a) Michigan State
b) Michigan
c) Purdue
d) Iowa

Question 166: A six-foot long, hand-carved canoe was originally donated by the city of Hollywood, Florida as a trophy for the winner of Miami's rivalry matchup with which school?
a) Florida State
b) Boston College
c) Virginia Tech
d) Florida

Question 167: Name the two players who have lettered for both Florida and Miami.

Question 168: In an effort to promote interest in the upcoming home matchup with Florida State, this Hurricane head coach flew to Tallahassee and held a "shadow boxing" match with FSU head coach Bobby Bowden.
a) Lou Saban
b) Dennis Erickson
c) Howard Schnellenberger
d) Fran Curci

Question 169: True or False: Defensive end Anthony Chickillo is a third-generation player for Miami.

Question 170: Randy Shannon won national championships as both a player and a coach. In which year was Shannon *not* present for a Miami national championship?
a) 1987
b) 1989
c) 1991
d) 2001

Question 171: This former Miami assistant coach was well known for his contempt for the Florida Gators. During the Florida game week, he would mockingly act and walk like a gator. Who is he?
a) Walt Kichefski

b) Armand "Stitch" Vari

c) Don Soldinger

d) Tom Olivadotti

Question 172: In 1972, Miami was the beneficiary of a rules error. Trailing 21-17 with less than a minute to play and facing fourth and 24, Canes QB Ed Carney's pass fell incomplete. However, the officials gave the Canes a fifth down, and Carney connected with Witt Beckman for a 32-yard score that gave Miami a controversial 24-21 win. Who was the opponent?

a) Florida

b) Rutgers

c) Tulane

d) Georgia Tech

Question 173: Which of the following defensive linemen did *not* earn All-American honors while at UM?

a) Don Latimer

b) Vince Wilfork

c) Eddie Edwards

d) Tony Cristiani

Question 174: In addition to wreaking havoc on the football field, Vince Wilfork also set the Miami indoor track school record for which event?

a) Hammer throw

b) Javelin toss

c) Discus throw

d) Shot put

Question 175: In which of the following comeback victories did Miami face the biggest deficit?

a) 1978 at Florida – 22-21 win

b) 2012 at Georgia Tech – 42-36 OT win

c) 1987 at Florida State – 26-25 win

d) 2003 vs. Florida – 38-33 win

Question 176: This Hurricane found the end zone twice in the first quarter as Miami jumped out to a 17-0 lead in the 1984 Orange Bowl.
  a) Alonzo Highsmith
  b) Albert Bentley
  c) Glenn Dennison
  d) Eddie Brown

Question 177: True or False: The 1983 Miami squad is the last national champion to win the title after losing its first game of the year (a 28-3 loss to Florida).

Question 178: How many former Hurricanes have been the #1 overall pick of the NFL Draft?
  a) 2
  b) 3
  c) 4
  d) 5

Question 179: Miami holds the NCAA record for most consecutive games without a tie, beginning in 1968 and spanning until the implementation of overtime in 1996. How many games does that streak span?
  a) 292
  b) 309
  c) 331
  d) 345

Question 180: This former Miami kicker shares an NCAA record for most games with a field goal being the winning margin of victory (ten times). Who is he?
  a) Carlos Huerta
  b) Todd Sievers
  c) Danny Miller
  d) Andy Prewitt

SECOND HALF ANSWER KEY
(161-180)

161. True – Gustafson was 9-7 vs. Florida in his career
162. Ted Hendricks
163. B
164. A
165. C
166. D
167. Phil Kaplan, Brock Berlin
168. C
169. True (Grandfather Nick: 1st-team All-American in '50s; father Tony played 1979-82)
170. B
171. A
172. C
173. B
174. D
175. D
176. C
177. True
178. A
179. D
180. C

Question 181: Which of the following Miami head coaches was the oldest when he took over the position?
a) Butch Davis
b) Larry Coker
c) Fran Curci
d) Howard Schnellenberger

Question 182: Houston Cougars' QB David Klingler had an epic season in 1990, throwing an NCAA-record 54 touchdown passes. It was a rude awakening for Klingler and his run-and-shoot offense the following year in the Orange Bowl, as Miami pounded the Cougars 40-10. How many times did the Miami defense sack the record-setting signal caller?
a) 4
b) 5
c) 6
d) 7

Question 183: In what year did the Canes and Gators play the final game of their *annual* series?
a) 1986
b) 1987
c) 1988
d) 1989

Question 184: Before Sebastian, what was the first mascot of the University of Miami to appear on the sidelines?

Question 185: When did the tradition of players taking the field through the smoke start?
a) 1940s
b) 1950s
c) 1960s
d) 1970s

Question 186: In which year did Miami defeat the AP #1 and #2 teams and *not* win the national championship?
a) 1986
b) 1990
c) 2000
d) 2002

Question 187: Which national championship-winning quarterback wore jersey number "4" at Miami?
a) Steve Walsh
b) Craig Erickson
c) Bernie Kosar
d) Gino Torretta

Question 188: RB Alonzo Highsmith was selected third overall in the 1987 NFL draft by which team?
a) Dallas Cowboys
b) Tampa Bay Buccaneers
c) Houston Oilers
d) New Orleans Saints

Question 189: With seconds remaining in the 2003 Fiesta Bowl / National Championship Game, Todd Sievers nailed a field goal to send the game into overtime. How long was the kick?
a) 30 yards
b) 33 yards
c) 40 yards
d) 47 yards

Question 190: How many former Canes were on the roster of the 1993-94 Super Bowl Champion Dallas Cowboys?
a) 3
b) 5
c) 6
d) 9

Question 191: Under Schnellenberger, Miami snapped a string of ten straight losses to Notre Dame. In what year did they finally break the streak?
a) 1980
b) 1981
c) 1982
d) 1983

Question 192: During which national championship season did Miami start the year with a 31-3 win at Arkansas?
a) 1987
b) 1991
c) 1983
d) 1989

Question 193: True or False: Brock Berlin ended his college career with a Peach Bowl victory over the Florida Gators.

Question 194: Which team with a winning all-time record against the Canes has beaten Miami the most times in school history?
a) Georgia Tech
b) Penn State
c) Alabama
d) Notre Dame

Question 195: Lou Saban's final career game as UM head coach was a 22-21 comeback victory against which team?
a) Notre Dame
b) Florida
c) Syracuse
d) Tulane

Question 196: The Canes won the 1980 Peach Bowl over Virginia Tech, marking their first bowl game appearance since which season?

a) 1972
b) 1975
c) 1967
d) 1959

Question 197: True or False: Fran Curci and Walt Kichefski combined to coach the 1970 season.

Question 198: Who did Jimmy Johnson beat for his first win as Miami's head coach?
a) Florida
b) Auburn
c) Purdue
d) Rice

Question 199: Miami has played in the Orange Bowl game a school-high nine times. In what year did they first play in the game?
a) 1933
b) 1935
c) 1946
d) 1951

Question 200: Which of the following was not a part of the "Melting Pot" offensive line from the 1983 championship team?
a) Ian Sinclair
b) Juan Comendeiro
c) Paul Bertucelli
d) Sherko Haji-Rasouli

SECOND HALF ANSWER KEY
(181-200)

181. B
182. B
183. B
184. An American Bulldog named Hurricane I
185. B
186. C
187. A
188. C
189. C
190. C
191. B
192. B
193. True
194. D
195. B
196. C
197. False – Charlie Tate coached the first 2 games, and
      Kichefski coached out the remainder of the season
198. B
199. B
200. D

THE RESULTS

Well, so let's see how you did. Are you bound for the UM Ring of (Trivia) Honor, or better served grilling steaks, shotgunning beers, and misquoting stats to your buddies at a September tailgate at Sun Life Stadium?

160-200 =
UM Ring of Honor

140-159 =
First-Team All-American

120-139=
UM Letterman

100-119 =
Practice Squad Member

0-99 =
You must be a Seminole!

ABOUT THE AUTHOR

Craig T. Smith is a practicing attorney who earned his law degree from the University of Miami after receiving an undergraduate degree from the University of Tennessee. He was fortunate enough to witness first-hand as a student one of the finest collections of college football talent in history in the 2001 Miami squad, and has since been mesmerized by the swagger and decades of dominance by the U.

Craig also hosted a weekend radio show on ESPN 1040 am Tampa Bay for over two years, and was a credentialed reporter covering the Tampa Bay Buccaneers for the station for the past three seasons. He presently writes about the Canes for SB Nation.

Craig lives in Tampa with his wife, Jennifer. This is his first book.

REFERENCES

Websites:

Hurricanesports.com
Umsportshalloffame.com
OrangeBowl.org
Miami.edu
Espn.com
Sportsillustrated.cnn.com
La84.org
Football-almanac.com
Sports-reference.com
fs.ncaa.org/Docs/stats/football_records
MiamiNewTimes.com
FamousQuotes.com
SearchQuotes.com

Books:

Martz, Jim. Tales from the Miami Hurricane sideline: a
        collection of the greatest Hurricane stories ever told.
        New York: Sports Pub, 2012.

Visit us on the web to learn more about Black Mesa and our authors:

www.blackmesabooks.com

Or contact us via email:

admin@blackmesabooks.com

54762894R00046

Made in the USA
Middletown, DE
06 December 2017